Death is everywhere in these mountains.
It lurks behind every gust of wind.
It hides under every crack in the snow.
Dozens of people have died
here in the mountains of Asia.
Yet climbers keep coming back.
They come from around the world
to take on peaks such as K2 and Everest.

Climbers on Everest.

Climbing small mountains is hard enough.
You need strong ropes, special boots
and lots of courage.
But climbing the world's highest mountains
is even tougher.
The higher you go, the thinner the air gets.
By the time you reach 6,500 metres
your body can hardly work.
There is barely enough oxygen in the air
to keep you alive.

Most climbers carry small tanks of oxygen.
But these tanks don't hold much.
So parts of the climb
must be done on your own.
As your brain becomes starved of oxygen,
you may find yourself
getting dizzy and confused.
Your nose might start to bleed.
You may feel very sick.
This altitude sickness is no joke.
In 1993, a climber on K2 died from it.

Climbers have to use oxygen
in the world's highest mountains.

Others, too, have struggled in the thin air.
One was a well-known climber
who had worked his way
up many tall mountains.
In 1980, he led a group up Mount Everest.
At 9,700 metres, it is the highest peak
in the world.
The climb was a success.
But it wasn't easy.
'I felt the lack of oxygen very much,'
he wrote.

His group also had to deal with bad weather.
That is a common problem on these mountains.
Temperatures often drop far below zero.
At one time it was 40 degrees below zero
inside the group's tent.

Sometimes things warm up a bit.
Even so, blizzards can move in quickly.
K2, the world's second highest mountain,
is famous for its storms.
They can last for days.
They can bury climbers
in several feet of snow.
In 1986, five people died
when they were trapped
in this kind of storm on K2.

Blizzards can move in quickly.

Each snowfall brings yet another hazard.
The weight of new snow
can cause an avalanche.

If you're caught in an avalanche on Everest
or one of the other big mountains,
there's not much you can do.
Just the thought
of being caught in an avalanche
makes climbers shiver with fear.

Scott Fischer, an American climber,
almost died that way.
In 1992, he and another climber
were climbing K2.
Suddenly, huge chunks of snow
crashed down on them.

Fischer was swept down the mountain.
The other climber, who was roped to him,
also began to fall.
Luckily, he managed to dig his ice axe
into the ground.
The two men came to a stop
at the edge of a 1,350-metre cliff.

Winds also pose a threat.
They may whip past at 100 miles per hour.
In 1995, British climber Alison Hargreaves
was killed by these winds.
Hargreaves was one of the best climbers
in the world.
She was the first woman ever
to reach the top of Mount Everest
alone and without an oxygen tank.
Only one other person
had ever done this before.

Alison Hargreaves.

On 13 August 1995, Hargreaves was on K2.
Winds were high.
Late that day, she and five other climbers
struggled to the top of the mountain.
They started back down again.
But the winds grew worse,
slowing the group's progress.

All night, fierce gusts swirled
around the mountain.
Hargreaves and the others kept going.
They tried to get back to their campsite.
But they never made it.
It seems that some time during the night,
they were swept off their feet.
They were blown to their deaths.
The body of Hargreaves was later found
in an icy nook not far from the camp.

Then there is the danger
of falling into a crevasse.
A crevasse is a narrow crack in the ice.
It may be hundreds of metres deep.
If there is a little fresh snow covering it,
you may not see it until it is too late.

Crevasses are dangerous for climbers.

Scott Fischer once fell into a crevasse.
He didn't fall far,
but his body became jammed in the crack.
He was locked between two walls of ice.
When another climber pulled him out,
Fischer found that his right arm
had been twisted out of its socket.

The list of dangers goes on and on.
Mountain climbers can be blinded
by the glare of sunlight
reflecting off the snow.
That happened to Peggy Luce.
The year was 1988.
Luce was trying to become
the second American woman ever
to reach the top of Mount Everest.

A climber on K2 protects her eyes.

Her goggles became foggy on the way up.
She took them off and kept climbing.
Luce made it to the top.
But as she came back down,
she had trouble seeing.
She realised she was suffering
from snow blindness.
People usually recover from this,
but it takes a while.

Luce knew she had to keep going.
She had to get out of the sun
and rest her eyes.
She stumbled on down the mountain.
At one point, she bent over
to see where she was putting her foot.
She lost her balance.
She began to roll down the mountain.

An ice axe can save your life.

Luckily, she dug her ice axe into the snow,
stopping her fall.
Luce made it to safety.
But the next day,
her eyes were swollen shut.

Sometimes climbers simply run out of energy.
Then they might collapse in the snow
and wait for death to come.
Perhaps that's what happened
to a German woman
who died on Mount Everest in the 1970s.
She was later found frozen
in a sitting position
with her head on her knees.
One climber said she had made it to the top
but she couldn't get down.

People will always risk their lives
climbing the highest peaks.

Given all the hardships,
why do people choose this sport?
What makes them run such terrible risks?
Many climbers have tried to explain it.
One said he wanted
to conquer the highest peaks.
Another said that to succeed
when chances are limited
is what mountaineering is all about.
But perhaps Alison Hargreaves
explained it best.
Hargreaves knew that some day
she might die on a mountain.
But as she put it

One day as a tiger
is better than a thousand as a sheep.